OSLO NORWAY

Travel Guide

2024

The Ultimate Oslo Guide to Exploring the City Like a Local, plus Cuisine, a 7-Day Itinerary Plan, Top Attractions, and much more

Susanna Clockfield

Oslo Norway Travel Guide 2024

The Ultimate Oslo Guide to Exploring the City Like a Local, plus Cuisine, a 7-Day Itinerary Plan, Top Attractions, and much more

Copyright

Table of Contents

Introduction

I couldn't help but wonder as I strolled through the bustling streets of Oslo, Norway, at the city's rich history and modern charm. One lovely afternoon, I decided to visit the Royal Palace, which is a must-see for each traveler. As I approached, I noticed Erik, a nice local tour guide who provided an interesting insight on the palace's history.

Erik, an Oslo native, gave fascinating stories about the Norwegian royal family and their ties to the city. He spoke passionately about King Harald V's reign and his deep cultural ties to Oslo. Erik's narration transported us back in time, bringing regal events and festivities to life with anecdotes.

Erik recommended a hidden gem after the tour: a quiet café nestled away in a medieval lane. He shared personal memories of growing up in Oslo over cups of creamy Norwegian coffee, giving me a genuine sense of the city's warmth and community.

My day in Oslo was more than just a sightseeing excursion; it was an immersion into its history and the warmth of its people, leaving me with cherished memories of this wonderful Norwegian capital.

Oslo, Norway's capital, embodies the spirit of Scandinavian adventure. As an adventurer who has explored every corner and crevice, I can speak to the innumerable treasures it has to offer tourists.

My journey began with a visit to the famed Vigeland Park, which is home to over 200 intriguing sculptures by Gustav Vigeland. I was amazed at the genuine portrayals of human emotion as I strolled through the wonderfully landscaped gardens, all set against the breathtaking backdrop of Oslo's greenery.

I went to the Viking Ship Museum to get a flavor of Norway's seafaring history. Looking at the magnificently preserved Viking ships, I felt transported back in time, visualizing the mighty warriors who once sailed these warships. The museum's rich exhibitions shed light on Viking era customs and legends, making it an instructive and entertaining experience.

The natural splendor of Oslo urged me to investigate deeper, so I went to the Oslofjord. A ferry voyage afforded spectacular views of the city's skyline, tucked amid rolling hills and clean seas. The various islands dotting the fjord are ideal for hiking and picnicking, allowing visitors to enjoy Oslo's gorgeous views.

In my search for cultural enrichment, I visited the Munch Museum, which is dedicated to the works of the renowned Norwegian artist Edvard Munch. His classic artwork, "The Scream," is housed here, attracting art fans from all over the world. The museum's rich collection provides a peek into Munch's progress as an artist, leaving me tremendously impressed.

No trip to Oslo would be complete without experiencing its gastronomic pleasures. The city's food scene reflects its eclectic culture, including traditional delicacies like gravlax and reindeer alongside cosmopolitan cuisines. A visit to Mathallen Oslo, a bustling food hall, allowed me to enjoy a cornucopia of flavors, from exquisite cheeses to gourmet chocolates.

I visited the Oslo Opera House to experience the city's modernity. The marble-clad roof of the structure, designed to imitate a glacier emerging from the fjord, is a popular site for panoramic views of the city. I ascended the building, taking in the breathtaking views of Oslo's skyline and the surrounding natural splendor.

A vacation to Oslo would be incomplete without learning about its marine history. The Norwegian marine Museum, located on the

Bygdoy Peninsula, takes tourists on a marine trip through the years. I was delighted at old ships, navigational tools, and exhibits highlighting Norway's seafaring heritage.

The Oslo Botanical Garden is a haven of peace for those seeking it. While strolling around the perfectly maintained gardens, I came across a diverse range of plant species from around the world. It's a peaceful haven away from the city's hustle and bustle, ideal for introspection and relaxation.

Oslo is a city that flawlessly integrates its rich past with modernity while being surrounded by nature's splendor. My intrepid discovery of this Scandinavian jewel left me with cherished memories and a profound appreciation for its cultural legacy and natural beauty. Whether you're a history buff, an art lover, a nature lover, or a foodie, Oslo has something extraordinary to offer any tourist seeking adventure and discovery.

- When to Visit

Oslo, Norway's dynamic city, offers a rich tapestry of experiences throughout the year, making it an attractive tourist destination. The optimal time to visit Oslo is determined by your tastes and the activities you wish to participate in.

Summer (June-August): This is the busiest tourist season in Oslo, when the city is at its most appealing. With temperatures ranging from 15°C to 25°C (59°F to 77°F), the weather is pleasant. The city's outdoor attractions, such as Vigeland Park, the Royal Palace, and the Oslo Fjord, are well-served by the city's long days with nearly 24 hours of daylight.

Cultural vibrancy is increased via festivals and events such as the Oslo Jazz Festival and the Mela Festival.

Autumn (September-October) and Spring (April-May): These shoulder seasons provide a good blend of pleasant weather and less visitors. Spring gives blossoms to the city's parks, while autumn colors the trees. It's a beautiful time to go trekking in the neighboring forests and take in the beauty.

Winter (December-February): Oslo is a winter sports enthusiast's ideal location. While the days are short and chilly, the city transforms into a winter wonderland, with the Northern Lights visible in adjacent places. Skiing, ice skating, and visiting Christmas markets are among the activities available.

Off-Peak (November and March): These months are the least busy, giving them a good value for money. Be prepared, however, for colder weather and shorter daylight hours.

Finally, the best time to visit Oslo is determined by your interests and weather tolerance. Whether you're looking for outdoor activities or cultural immersion, Oslo has something for you all year.

I had the great opportunity to visit Oslo, Norway, during the winter season a few years ago. It was a journey packed with icy vistas, enchanting city lights, and the pleasure of discovering a true Nordic winter wonderland.

I arrived in Oslo in early December, just as the city was getting into the festive spirit. Twinkling lights decorated the streets, and the aroma of freshly cooked pastries drifted from snug cafés. What piqued my interest the most, however, was the potential of enjoying Norway's renowned winter activities.

My first adventure took me to the world-famous Holmenkollen Ski Jump. Standing at the top of the ski jump, I took in the panoramic views of Oslo below, which was completely blanketed in snow. I also got to try cross-country skiing, drifting through the city's gorgeous forests.

I went on a Northern Lights tour with a local guide one evening. We traveled out of town to a rural location with little light pollution. Nature repaid us with a beautiful show of the Northern Lights dancing over the Arctic heavens as we stood there in the bitter cold, gazing up at the night sky. It was both bizarre and humbling.

To warm up, I visited the Viking Ship Museum and the Munch Museum in Oslo, immersing myself in Norway's rich history and art. Of course, I ate great Norwegian food, savoring heavy meals like reindeer stew and warm, comforting bowls of fish soup.

As my trip came to a conclusion, I couldn't help but think about how magical Oslo is in the winter. It was an adventure and a cozy journey when I discovered the true spirit of Norwegian culture in the midst of snow and sparkling lights. Oslo's winter had enchanted me, leaving me with fond recollections of this lovely city.

Let us go on a journey together, with empathy for your excitement and curiosity about what lies ahead.

The Oslo Card:

Begin your journey with the Oslo Card, your golden ticket to convenience. This card provides access to all modes of public transit, including buses, trams, ferries, and the metro. It's a key to Oslo's heart, allowing you to easily immerse yourself in its wonders.

Trams and buses:

Oslo's trams and buses are lifelines that run across the city's neighborhoods. Riding them with residents will allow you to feel the pulse of the city. Tram line 12 winds through the picturesque streets of Grünerlkka, a region brimming with art, culture, and fashionable cafes.

The Oslo Metro:

Descend into the city's underground world, the Oslo Metro, also known as the T-bane. Remember that beneath the surface of the city is a city full of surprises as you ride through tunnels filled with stunning artwork.

Ferries:

The heart of Oslo is entwined with the fjords. Take the ferry to the Peninsula, where the Viking Ship Museum and the Fram Museum bring history to life. Set sail towards the Oslo Islands, a hidden jewel where nature's tranquility meets the hustle and bustle of city life.

Walking and bicycling:

For the more daring, Oslo has beautiful walking and biking trails. Stroll along the Aker Brygge promenade, take in some street art in the Greenland area, or ride your bike through beautiful parks like Vigelandsparken, a sculpture lover's paradise.

Electric Scooters:

Oslo is environmentally sensitive and supports electric scooters. Explore hidden places while zipping through the city with the wind in your hair.

Taxis and rideshares:

When the desire for comfort strikes, taxis and rideshares are readily available. Engage with nice drivers who can give local knowledge.

Embrace the "Slow Travel" Mindset: Finally, Oslo is about enjoying the journey rather than the destination. Slow down, take in the scenery, and let Oslo unfold before you.

As you navigate Oslo's streets and rivers, keep in mind that you are becoming a part of the city's story, one of innovation, nature, and the warm embrace of Norwegian culture. Enjoy every second of this fantastic journey.

Visa Requirements

Tourist Visa Requirements in Oslo, Norway

Oslo, Norway's capital, is an enthralling destination recognized for its breathtaking natural surroundings, rich cultural legacy, and dynamic metropolitan life. If you're considering a tourist trip to Oslo, knowing the visa requirements is critical to ensuring a pleasant and trouble-free vacation.

Visa Waivers:

Citizens of the European Union (EU) and the European Free Trade Association (EFTA) do not require a visa to visit Norway, including Oslo, for short stays of up to 90 days.

Visa-free travel for tourists is also available to nationals of the United States and Canada.

Norway is a part of the Schengen Area, which allows visitors to roam freely between 26 European countries with a single visa.

Visa Categories:

Tourist Visa (Schengen Visa): For short visits in Oslo, most tourists will apply for a Schengen Visa. It enables you to visit Oslo and other Schengen countries.

If you intend to visit Oslo more than once during your vacation, you need to apply for a multiple-entry visa.

Procedure for Applying:

To begin your visa application, go to the Norwegian Embassy or Consulate in your home country, or utilize the online application portal.

Fill out the application form and gather the necessary documents, which include a valid passport, proof of travel insurance, a flight schedule, and a reservation for lodging.

Pay the visa cost and, if necessary, attend an interview.

Visa processing periods vary, but they normally take 15 calendar days. It is best to apply well in advance of your departure date.

Stay Duration: With a Schengen Visa, you can stay in Oslo for up to 90 days within a 180-day period.

Visa Extenders: Schengen visas cannot be extended. If you want to stay for a longer period of time, you must leave the Schengen Area and apply for a new visa.

The visa charge varies according to your age, nationality, and type of visa. For the most up-to-date fee information, see the official website.

Border Protection:

You may be subject to passport and visa inspections upon arrival in Oslo. Make sure you have all of the appropriate documentation.

Remember that visa requirements sometimes vary, so make sure to check the most up-to-date information on the official website of the Norwegian Embassy or Consulate in your country before arranging a trip to Oslo, Norway. A little planning ahead of time will help you make the most of your vacation to this charming Scandinavian city.

Let me tell you about an incredible personal experience I had on my trip to Oslo.

As an intrepid traveler, I set out for Oslo, Norway, with the goal of discovering the rough landscapes and immersing myself in the enchanting culture of this Scandinavian treasure. As I stepped off the plane and into the cool Norwegian air, my heart raced. I had no idea my adventure would take such a fantastic turn.

I began my exploration of Oslo's bustling streets and historical monuments with my rucksack and camera in tow. Every part of the city contained a new and enthralling narrative, from the famed Vigeland Park, adorned with Gustav Vigeland's stunning sculptures, to the grandiose Oslo Opera House, which seemed to emerge from the fjord like an iceberg.

My true experience, though, awaited me on the outskirts of Oslo. I chose to tackle the well-known Trolltunga path, a 22-kilometer trek noted for its spectacular views and difficult terrain. The voyage to the Troll's Tongue was both physically and mentally challenging. The path wound through lush forests, rocky terrain, and gurgling streams, challenging my endurance at every turn.

It was an emotional achievement to reach the Trolltunga viewpoint. I felt a great connection to Norway's untamed beauty as I stood on that famed rock, jutting out over a 700-meter plunge to Lake Ringedalsvatnet. It was an adventurer's dream realized, a moment when time appeared to stop.

But here's where my adventure story takes a turn. The weather suddenly became bad on my journey back from Trolltunga. Dark clouds moved in, and a steady downpour began. My pulse was hammering with each step as I navigated treacherous rocks and muddy pathways. The peaceful setting had been changed into a daunting struggle.

I understood I was lost when the light faded. Panic welled up within me, but I knew I had to keep my cool. I retraced my tracks, aided by my survival instincts and a reliable map. After hours of searching, I came across a trail marker. I felt a wave of relief flood over me.

I made it back to my starting position, exhausted and drenched. The journey had taken an unexpected turn, but it had also taught me resilience, flexibility, and the raw power of nature. Despite the difficulties, I wouldn't trade my Oslo experience for anything. It was a journey that pushed my boundaries, rewarded my spirit, and left me with a story to remember for the rest of my life.

Chapter 1: 7 Best Top Attractions

While exploring this Scandinavian treasure, you'll come across a wealth of sights that will captivate your senses and leave you with amazing memories. I'll take you on a tour of seven of Oslo's best top attractions, sharing personal anecdotes and experiences along the way.

Our adventure begins at Vigeland Park, a large green paradise in the middle of Oslo. This one-of-a-kind sculpture park features over 200 magnificent bronze and granite monuments by renowned Norwegian artist Gustav Vigeland. Every statue tells a different narrative, but my personal favorite is the classic "Angry Boy," whose stubborn face has long piqued my interest. As you go through the park, you will see the craftsmanship and emotion that each sculpture exudes.

The Viking Ship Museum: If you want to learn more about Norway's Viking heritage, I recommend paying a visit to the Viking Ship Museum. Stepping into this museum is like stepping back in time, where you'll be amazed by the remarkably well-preserved Viking longships, especially the Oseberg ship.

I recall standing in front of this magnificent ship, admiring its complex carvings and fantasizing about the adventurous adventures of the Viking mariners who previously sailed on her.

The Oslo Opera House: An architectural marvel, the Oslo Opera House is a symbol of modernity in Norway. Its sloping top, which allows guests to stroll up and enjoy panoramic views of the city, distinguishes it. One beautiful afternoon, I joined locals and tourists in ascending the roof, and the view of Oslo's cityscape paired with the fjord was stunning. Holmenkollen Ski Museum and Tower: Holmenkollen Ski Museum and Tower is a must-see for an adrenaline rush and a dose of history.

I remember the thrill of riding the elevator to the top of the ski jump tower and looking down at the enormous slope that has held numerous skiing contests. The interactive exhibits within the museum shed information on the origins of skiing, and the view from the summit provides a beautiful vista of Oslo.

Akershus Fortress: Akershus Fortress, which has guarded Oslo's harbor for centuries, is a must-see for history fans. I felt transported back in time as I walked along the ancient walls. Inside, the Resistance Museum portrays the riveting story of Norway's WWII battle, inspiring deep admiration for the Norwegian people's fortitude.

The Munch Museum: Art lovers will appreciate the Munch Museum, which is dedicated to the works of the famed Norwegian painter Edvard Munch. The highlight is, without a question, Munch's renowned masterwork "The Scream." I was astounded to see the actual painting in person, as I was astonished at the strength of emotion communicated via the artwork.

The Fram Museum: To cap off our Oslo tour, the Fram Museum provides a one-of-a-kind experience. You may visit the polar expedition vessel Fram, which was utilized by great explorers such as Roald Amundsen. I recall standing in the cabin of this old ship, thinking of the harsh conditions these daring explorers faced while pushing the bounds of human exploration.

Finally, the greatest attractions in Oslo weave a complex tapestry of history, art, and natural beauty. My own experiences in this enthralling city have left an unforgettable impact on me, and I hope your tour through these enthralling locations is equally rewarding. Oslo is a city that perfectly blends its past and present, providing every visitor with a memorable experience.

Getting to These destinations

The city's efficient and well-connected transit infrastructure makes it easy to get about the city's key attractions. Here's an overview of how to get around these areas:

Walking: Many of Oslo's attractions, such as Vigeland Park, the Oslo Opera House, and Akershus Fortress, are conveniently located in the city center and can be reached on foot. Strolling about the city is a terrific opportunity to absorb the local culture while also discovering hidden gems along the route.

Oslo has an extensive public transportation network, mostly trams, buses, and the metro. Tickets for all kinds of public transportation can be purchased through vending machines or the Ruter smartphone app. The city's public transportation system is clean, safe, and on time, making it an excellent option for traveling around.

Cycling: With dedicated bike lanes and bike-sharing schemes, Oslo is a bike-friendly city. You can rent a bike from a variety of sites around town and explore at your own leisure. It's an excellent method to go to places like Vigeland Park, the Viking Ship Museum, and the Munch Museum.

Taxis: Taxis in Oslo are trustworthy, but they are more expensive than public transportation. They are easily accessible at taxi stands or by hailing one on the street. If you choose not to take public transportation, taxis are a simple way to get to sights like the Holmenkollen Ski Museum and Tower.

Ferries: Because Oslo is located along the Oslo Fjord, ferries are a fun way to go to some of the city's attractions. For example, you can take a ferry to the Bygdy Peninsula, which houses the Viking Ship Museum, the Fram Museum, and other museums. Views from the ferry are an added bonus!

Hop-On Hop-Off Tours: If you prefer a guided tour of Oslo's sights, a hop-on-hop-off bus trip is an option. These tours often cover all of the key attractions, giving you the freedom to explore at your own leisure while listening to interesting commentary.

Car Rentals: While not required for getting around the city center, renting a car is an option if you want to explore the outskirts of Oslo or go on day trips to adjacent locations. Just keep in mind that parking in the city center might be pricey and difficult to locate.

- Grünerløkka

Grünerlkka, sometimes known as "Lkka" by locals, is one of Oslo's most active and distinct neighborhoods. This former industrial district, located just northeast of the city center, has been turned into a trendy center for art, culture, and innovation. Follow these tourist recommendations to thoroughly immerse yourself in the spirit of Grünerlkka.

Getting There:

Grünerlkka is easily accessible thanks to Oslo's effective public transportation system. Begin by taking the T-bane (subway) to the Thorshovgata or Nybrua stations on the Grünerlkka line (Line 11). These stations are centrally located, providing easy access to the surrounding area.

Trams and buses: Trams 11, 12, and 13 stop in Grünerlkka, as do buses 30 and 31. This allows you the freedom to choose the path that best suits your starting place.

Exploring Grünerlkka: Graffiti and Street Art: Begin your trip with a stroll through the bright streets filled with vivid murals and street art. The neighborhood is well-known for its ever-changing outdoor art gallery, which features the work of both local and foreign artists.

Grünerlkka has a profusion of unique boutiques, vintage stores, and artisan businesses. As you stroll through its picturesque streets, look for one-of-a-kind fashion items, handmade crafts, and fashionable homeware.

Markets: On weekends, don't miss the Grünerlkka Loppemarked (flea market) along Birkelunden Park. You'll come across vintage treasures, antiques, and odd oddities. Alternatively, the Mathallen Oslo food hall is a foodie's delight, serving a wide variety of Norwegian and international dishes.

Cafés and eateries: Grünerlkka is home to some of Oslo's top cafés and eateries. Tim Wendelboe's café serves great coffee, and Café Fedora serves traditional Norwegian cuisine. Explore the different food alternatives that line the streets for a more multicultural experience.

Parks & Green Spaces: Take a break in one of Grünerlkka's verdant oases. Park life is an important element of the neighborhood's appeal, with parks such Olaf Ryes Plass and

Sofienbergparken providing great sites for picnics or a leisurely read.

Music and Nightlife: In the evening, Grünerlkka comes alive with a bustling music and nightlife scene. Check out Bl, a well-known club featuring live music performances, or have a drink at one of the many bars in the area.

Local Culture: To learn more about local culture, go to the Anker Brewery, a historic landmark that today includes art galleries, boutiques, and restaurants. It is a prime illustration of Grünerlkka's metamorphosis from an industrial district to a cultural destination.

Grünerlkka's bohemian vibe, creative flair, and numerous offerings make it a must-see location in Oslo. Whether you're drawn to its creative energy, gastronomic delights, or cultural attractions, you'll discover that this area captures the soul of modern Oslo, making your stay an unforgettable experience. Set aside a day to explore Grünerlkka, and you'll discover a bright and active side of the Norwegian city that is not to be missed.

Frogner Park is the largest park in Oslo, Norway, and it is home to the world-renowned Vigeland Sculpture Park. The park is a must-see for any tourist to Oslo and is noted for its over 200 bronze, granite, and cast iron sculptures by Norwegian sculptor Gustav Vigeland. The sculptures portray the human body in all periods of life, from birth to death, and are a strong and compelling statement of the human experience.

The park is separated into sections, each with its unique theme. The Monolith is a towering column of 121 human figures portraying the cycle of life. The Wheel of Life is a circular fountain with 140 statues reflecting the various stages of life. The Sinnataggen is a prominent sculpture in the park depicting a naked boy violently kicking his foot.

The park also has a playground, a café, and a restaurant. It is a popular site for both locals and tourists, and it is a terrific place to relax and enjoy the outdoors.

My personal experience exploring Frogner Park was fantastic. The magnitude and beauty of the sculptures, as well as the way they reflected the human experience in such a raw and honest way, hit me. I spent hours roaming through the park, admiring the many sculptures and contemplating their significance.

The Monolith was one of the sculptures that really spoke to me. The towering column of figures was both awe-inspiring and humbling, and it made me reflect on the immensity of time and the interdependence of all life.

Sinnataggen was another sculpture that I admired. The angry child served as a reminder of the power of emotions and the significance of expressing them in a healthy manner.

Overall, my visit to Frogner Park was profound and poignant. It is a site I will never forget, and I highly suggest it to anyone visiting Oslo.

Here are some ideas for visiting Frogner Park:
Allow plenty of time to visit the park. There are nearly 200 sculptures, so you won't want to rush through it.
Wear comfy shoes. You'll be doing a lot of walking.

Bring a camera. You'll want to photograph all of the magnificent sculptures.

Visit during the summer months when the park is in full bloom.

Take a guided tour. This is an excellent method to learn more about the sculptures and the park's history.

.

- Majorstuen

Majorstuen, located in the center of Oslo, is a bustling and captivating area that draws visitors with its unique blend of culture, history, and modernity. As you enter this picturesque region, you'll be engulfed in a tapestry of experiences that will enchant you.

Here's a full tour of Majorstuen to make your vacation genuinely unforgettable.

Majorstuen's history dates back to the 19th century, when it was a little village on the outskirts of Oslo. It preserves its historical appeal today thanks to well-preserved architecture, such as the landmark Majorstuen Church, a Neo-Gothic masterpiece that bears witness to the district's rich history.

Shopping Paradise: Majorstuen is a shopaholic's dream. Begin your shopping spree on Bogstadveien, the district's major shopping street. There are numerous boutiques, worldwide names, and local designers. Don't miss the Sunday flea market at Birkelunden Park for one-of-a-kind items.

Visit The Vigeland Park, a short tram ride away, to immerse yourself in Majorstuen's cultural environment. Over 200 bronze and granite sculptures by renowned artist Gustav Vigeland can be found here. The Monolith, the park's centerpiece, is a towering marvel that takes visitors' breath away.

Epicurean Delights: The gastronomic scene in Majorstuen is a delectable combination of traditional Norwegian flavors and international cuisine. Kaffebrenneriet serves smbd (open-faced sandwiches), and Fiskeriet Youngstorget serves seafood. Pascal, a renowned patisserie, is the place to go for dessert.

Nature enthusiasts will appreciate Majorstuen's proximity to the Nordmarka forest. Hike the trails, have picnics beside Sognsvann Lake, or go cross-country skiing in the winter. The tranquility of the woodland stands in stark contrast to the hustle and bustle of the metropolis.

Architectural Wonders: Stroll through Majorstuen's charming streets and marvel at the unique mix of architectural styles, ranging from Jugendstil to modernist designs. The Royal Palace is nearby, and you may see the royal ritual of the Changing of the Guard.

Majorstuen's strategic position makes it an ideal starting point for exploring Oslo. Other downtown attractions such as the Opera House, Akershus Fortress, and the Viking Ship

Museum are easily accessible via tram and metro stations.

Majorstuen in Oslo, Norway, is a location that combines history, culture, and contemporary in a seamless manner. This area provides an exceptional experience for every traveler, whether you're strolling through its charming streets, sampling local foods, or immersing yourself in its cultural legacy.

My Trip to Majorstuen Oslo

I recall vividly the day I ventured out to discover Majorstuen in Oslo, Norway. The air was crisp, and there was a sense of adventure in the air. Majorstuen was my first stop on a European tour, and there was no better place to begin my voyage.

Majorstuen Church, an architectural gem that transported me back in time, was where I started my exploration. The church's

Neo-Gothic exterior and elaborate decorations were stunning. As I entered, I was greeted by a calm mood, and the soft light flowing through stained glass windows produced a surreal atmosphere.

I next walked into Majorstuen's busy core, Bogstadveien. The busy street was lined with shops and cafes, and I couldn't help but crave some Norwegian fare. I enjoyed a scrumptious smrbrd, a Norwegian open-faced sandwich, at Kaffebrenneriet. I was left wanting more because of the blend of flavors and textures.

Vigeland Park was the highlight of my day. I was captivated by the intense feelings and concepts represented in each of Gustav Vigeland's sculptures as I went among them. The Monolith, a colossal column of linked figures, inspired me. I spent hours in the park photographing and admiring the artwork.

In the evening, I dined at Fiskeriet Youngstorget, a local fish restaurant. The flavors of Norwegian cuisine and the freshness of the seafood were a revelation. I had a delicious supper while speaking with friendly people who told me stories and gave me advice for the rest of my trip.

As the sun began to set, I made my way to Nordmarka woodland, which was only a short tram ride away. The forest provided a peaceful respite from the city's rush and bustle. I went for a leisurely walk along a trail, and the peace of the woods engulfed me. It was the ideal way to round off my day in Majorstuen.

Majorstuen had not only exposed me to Oslo's rich history and culture, but he had also set the tone for the rest of my European journey. The memories of that day in this wonderful neighborhood linger, reminding me of the wonders of travel and the treasures hidden in every corner of the globe.

Aker Brygge

Aker Brygge is a vibrant waterfront neighborhood in the center of Oslo, Norway, known for its compelling mix of modernity and heritage. This dynamic district, nestled along the shores of the Oslo Fjord, has transformed over the years from an industrial shipyard to a flourishing hub for cultural, food, shopping, and leisure activities.

Aker Brygge's history extends back to the nineteenth century, when it housed the Aker Mekaniske Verksted shipyard, a symbol of Norway's nautical legacy. However, as shipbuilding declined in prominence, the area had a revival in the 1980s. Aker Brygge is now a great example of urban renovation, elegantly integrating old and new.

The gorgeous boardwalk that stretches down the fjord is one of Aker Brygge's most appealing features. It's ideal for leisurely strolls, with spectacular views of the ocean, boats, and the renowned Oslo Opera House. The waterfront promenade is lined with attractive outdoor cafes, making it a great spot for a cup of coffee or a meal while watching boats float by.

Exploring Aker Brygge is a must-do for foodies. The neighborhood is home to a vast range of restaurants serving cuisine ranging from traditional Norwegian dishes such as fresh seafood and reindeer to foreign delicacies. Don't miss out on classic Norwegian meals at Fjord Restaurant or a gourmet experience at Lofoten Fish Restaurant.

Aker Brygge is also a shopping haven, with a plethora of high-end boutiques, art galleries, and specialty shops. Everything from designer apparel and homemade crafts to Scandinavian interior design products can be found here, making it an ideal destination to pick up mementos or indulge in some retail therapy.

The Astrup Fearnley Museum of Modern Art is a must-see for everyone interested in contemporary art. Its eye-catching architecture and world-class collection of modern art draw visitors from all over the world.

As nighttime falls, Aker Brygge's lively nightlife comes to life. The area's pubs and clubs provide a wide range of beverages, live music, and entertainment, making it an ideal place to unwind and enjoy the city's dynamic nocturnal scene.

As I stepped off the train in Oslo, Norway, the fresh, invigorating Nordic air greeted me with the promise of adventure. Little did I realize that my voyage would take me to the lovely area of Gamle Oslo, where history and modernity coexist together, producing a mesmerizing experience for travelers.

Gamle Oslo, or "Old Oslo," is a tribute to the city's rich legacy and ongoing progress. The journey through this district begins with the magnificent Oslo Central Station, where old and new meet. Travelers like me are introduced to the city's unique blend of history and modernity.

A trip through Gamle Oslo's cobblestone streets is like stepping into a time machine. The region is home to some of Oslo's most prominent historical landmarks, including the ancient

Akershus Fortress. The stronghold guards the city and provides stunning views of Oslo's lovely port, which is frequently dotted with yachts. I was caught in the history of monarchs and conquerors that this castle has witnessed over the centuries.

I continued walking till I reached the attractive and vibrant district of Grünerlkka. With its art galleries, boutiques, and vibrant street art, this hipster paradise exemplifies Oslo's creative energy. Grünerlkka is the ideal place to have a cup of locally roasted coffee, indulge in traditional Norwegian pastries, or browse vintage boutiques that provide a one-of-a-kind shopping experience.

The Botanical Garden in Gamle Oslo is a sanctuary of natural beauty for people looking for peace and quiet in the midst of the city. Its well-kept gardens feature an astonishing assortment of flora, providing it a tranquil retreat from the city's bustle. The greenhouse, with its tropical environment, is especially intriguing, bringing guests to another dimension.

A trip to Gamle Oslo would be incomplete without seeing the Munch Museum, which is dedicated to the famed Norwegian artist Edvard Munch. His famous painting "The Scream," as well as a large collection of his other works, can be accessed here. It's an opportunity to delve into the depths of Munch's emotional craftsmanship and appreciate his contribution to the world of art.

As the sun sets over the Oslofjord, I find myself at the Oslo Opera House. Its futuristic design appears to rise from the ocean, and it is more than just a destination for opera fans. Visitors can reach the rooftop for panoramic views of the city and the fjord, providing a captivating contrast between the old and contemporary parts of Oslo.

Gamle Oslo, with its rich history, cultural diversity, and energetic atmosphere, is a tapestry of experiences that every traveler should explore. It's a site where the past meets the present, providing a look into the soul of Oslo, Norway's intriguing capital. Whether you're a history enthusiast, an art lover, or simply looking for the spirit of Norwegian living, Gamle Oslo guarantees a memorable adventure that transcends time and leaves an everlasting impact on your trip memories.

- Traditional Norwegian Cuisine

When visiting Norway, the stunning scenery of fjords and mountains are not the only treasures to be discovered. Norway's culinary legacy, which is profoundly entrenched in tradition and environment, provides a pleasant trip for any foodie. Traditional Norwegian food exemplifies the country's relationship to its natural surroundings, and it's an adventure you won't want to miss.

A Taste of Norwegian Tradition

Norwegian cuisine is influenced by millennia of living in peace with nature. Norwegians have a varied selection of ingredients that form the heart of their traditional recipes thanks to the sea, forests, and rich regions. Seafood, particularly salmon and cod, is one of the most famous parts of Norwegian cuisine. Fresh from the cold, pure waters, these fish are the stars of many Norwegian recipes.

The Art of the Open-Faced Sandwich

Your gastronomic journey around Norway begins with "smrbrd," an open-faced sandwich that highlights the simplicity and purity of Norwegian ingredients. These scrumptious dishes are made with rye bread and a variety of toppings such as cured meats, cheeses, and smoked salmon. Smbd is a feast for the eyes and the tongue that shows the country's commitment to quality, flavor, and aesthetics.

The Salmon's Magic

Norwegian salmon is known around the world for its remarkable flavor and quality. You can eat "gravlaks," thinly sliced cured salmon served with mustard sauce, or "rakfisk," a fermented salmon dish that takes some getting used to but is worth trying for its peculiar flavor.

Visit local fish markets and try freshly caught salmon for a genuinely authentic experience.

Visit a typical Norwegian "koldtbord," a big buffet including an array of foods highlighting the diversity of Norwegian cuisine, for an immersive gastronomic experience. A vast variety of fish, meats, cheeses, and pickled vegetables are available. Don't pass up the chance to try "lutefisk," a unique meal made from dried fish preserved in lye, or "torrfisk," a dried and salted fish that has been a family favorite for centuries.

Desserts & Sweet Treats

Norway's sweet delicacies are as enticing as its savory fare. Enjoy "lefse," a soft and thin potato flatbread that is commonly smeared with butter and sugar, or "klippfisk," a delectable dessert made from dried and sweetened cod. These pastries demonstrate the Norwegian proclivity for transforming ordinary ingredients into delectable treats.

The Aquavit Expedition

A culinary tour through Norway is not complete unless you try "aquavit," a traditional Norwegian liquor. Aquavit is a digestif that is distilled from potatoes or grain and infused with a variety of botanicals. Its unusual flavors, which range from caraway to dill, offer a distinct taste of Norway's culinary heritage.

You will not only nourish your body but also connect with the history, culture, and soul of this magnificent country as you experience the traditional flavors of Norwegian food. Each dish tells a tale of a people who have prospered in one of the most beautiful yet difficult settings on the planet. So, embark on this culinary adventure and allow your taste sensations to guide you through the enthralling world of traditional Norwegian cuisine.

Allow me to tell you a personal anecdote about the beautiful experience of discovering traditional Norwegian cuisine.
I traveled to Norway last summer with the intention of immersing myself in the country's rich culture and magnificent surroundings. I had no idea that the culinary adventure that awaited me would be one of the most memorable portions of my vacation.
My first exposure with Norwegian cuisine occurred in a little seaside town, when I discovered a local restaurant serving traditional fare. I ordered a traditional "smbd" to get a taste of Norwegian cuisine. The plate's visual

appeal captured me when it came. A slice of substantial rye bread was topped with thinly sliced smoked salmon, vivid greens, and a dab of creamy mustard sauce. I felt like I was tasting the essence of Norway itself with each bite—fresh, clean, and in harmony with nature.

The next gastronomic adventure I couldn't pass up was a trip to a crowded fish market. I witnessed the beautiful tapestry of colors and flavors that comprise Norwegian fish here. As I relished the tastiest salmon sashimi I'd ever had, the aroma of the sea filled the air. It was as though the fish had leapt from the frigid waters directly onto my plate.

I had the honor of attending a traditional Norwegian "koldtbord" feast one evening. The buffet extended as far as the eye could see, a veritable feast of tastes. I tried everything, from delicate pickled herring to spicy "pinnekjott," or lamb ribs. Each bite highlighted Norwegian cuisine's time-honored culinary expertise and affection for local products.

Norway's desserts were similarly enticing. I recall eating "lefse," a sweet potato flatbread, while gazing out over the breathtaking fjords. Its silky texture combined with its remarkable natural beauty created an indelible impression.

But the most memorable experience of my culinary odyssey happened by happenstance in a rural village. I joined the people at a summer event, when they served me handmade "klippfisk." I loved this intriguing treat, prepared from dried and sweetened cod, while sitting around a bonfire. The flavors were unlike anything I'd ever tasted before—sweet and salty, a monument to the Norwegian people's ingenuity.

When I think back on my culinary trip in Norway, I realize it wasn't just about the food. It was about the stories that were intertwined with each dish, the connection to nature, and the kindness of the people who shared their traditions with me. Traditional Norwegian food is more than simply a dinner; it's a journey through history and culture that I will remember for the rest of my life.

The Top ten greatest restaurants in Oslo, Norway, for adventurous foodies:

Maaemo: Maaemo is a three-Michelin-starred restaurant in Oslo known for its Nordic cuisine. Seasonal, foraged, and expertly made cuisine highlighting the purity of Norwegian ingredients will delight adventurous guests.

Nedre Foss Grd: Nedre Foss Grd, located in a historic structure, serves a mix of traditional and modern Norwegian food.
Visitors can sample a meal that includes reindeer, elk, and seafood, all served with modern twists.

Statholdergaarden: Statholdergaarden is a historic mansion that serves authentic Norwegian food with a refined touch.

For a taste of Norway's culinary heritage, adventurous foodies can try lutefisk, whale steak, and cloudberries.

Smalhans: With its ever-changing, cheap three-course menu, Smalhans offers an intriguing voyage through Nordic cuisine.

It's ideal for individuals who wish to try a range of cuisine in a single visit.

Lofoten Fiskerestaurant: A must-visit for seafood fans, Lofoten Fiskerestaurant serves the freshest catch from Norway's coast.

Guests can dine on king crab legs and bacalao while taking in the nautical-inspired environment.

Vippa: Vippa is a waterfront dining hall ideal for adventurers seeking varied culinary experiences.

It offers a variety of flavors to discover, ranging from international street food to traditional Norwegian fare.

Funky Fresh Foods: With its inventive plant-based meals, this vegan eatery appeals to curious palates.

Guests can indulge in flavorful vegan sushi, raw sweets, and creative salads.

Olympen: Olympen is a historic beer hall that serves traditional Norwegian cuisine and a large selection of craft brews.

Reindeer stew, herring, and other robust meals can be sampled alongside local brews.

Pjoltergeist: Pjoltergeist is a daring blend of Nordic and South American cuisines that results in distinct flavors.

Dishes such as pickled shark and ceviche highlight the chef's creative approach.

Dognvill Burger Vulkan: Dognvill Burger Vulkan is the place to go if you're looking for a burger adventure.

They specialize in gourmet burgers with inventive toppings and flavor combinations.

When it comes to dining, explorers in Oslo are spoiled for choice. Whether you're looking for a sophisticated dining experience at Maaemo or experiencing street food at Vippa, these top ten restaurants offer a delightful gourmet tour into the heart of Norway's culinary traditions, making Oslo a true foodie paradise.

How to get around this restaurant and how much it costs every meal

Let's talk about how to go around these top restaurants in Oslo and estimate the cost per meal:

Maaemo: Location: Schweigaards gate 15b, 0191 Oslo, in the city center.

Maaemo's multi-course tasting menu costs roughly 2,500 to 3,000 Norwegian Krone (NOK) per person.

Nedre Foss Gård address i Torggata 16, 0181 Oslo.

Cost per lunch: A three-course lunch will cost you between 600 and 900 NOK per person.

Statholdergaarden can be found at Rådhusgata 11, 0151 Oslo.

Cost per lunch: A three-course lunch at Statholdergaarden might cost between 800 and 1,200 NOK per person.

Smalhans' adresse er Waldemar Thranes gate 10, 0171 Oslo.

Smalhans offers an economical three-course menu costing between 300 and 450 NOK per person.

Lofoten Fiskerestaurant is located at Observatoriegata 1B in Oslo, Norway.

Cost per Meal: Seafood lovers should plan on spending between 800 and 1,200 NOK per person for a meal here.

Vippa's address is Akershusstranda 25, 0150 Oslo.

Vippa is a food hall with diverse costs, but you may find meals for as little as 100 NOK or splurge on various cuisines.

Funky Fresh Foods is located in Underhaugsveien 2 in Oslo, Norway.

Cost per Meal: At Funky Fresh Foods, vegan pleasures range from 150 to 300 NOK per person.

Olympen is located at Grnland 15, 0188 Oslo.

A substantial supper at Olympen might cost between 350 and 600 NOK per person, including drinks.

Poltergeist can be found at Torggata 16, 0181 Oslo.

Cost per Meal: For a one-of-a-kind eating experience, budget between 700 and 1,000 NOK per person.

Dgnvill Burger Vulkan is located at Vulkan 8, 0178 Oslo.

Cost per Meal: Dognvill Burger Vulkan serves gourmet burgers with costs ranging from 200 to 300 NOK per person.

- Coffee shops and bars

Oslo, Norway, with its breathtaking fjords, rich history, and vibrant culture, has a plethora of tourist attractions. Among these are the city's attractive cafés and bars, which serve as welcoming havens for both inhabitants and visitors. Oslo has it all, whether you're looking for a peaceful setting to enjoy a cup of Norwegian coffee or a vibrant bar to experience the city's nightlife.

Cafés in Oslo include:

Wendelboe, Tim: Begin your day at Tim Wendelboe, an award-winning café recognized for its outstanding coffee. This café in Grünerlkka is a haven for coffee enthusiasts. The minimalist decor and welcoming ambiance make it the ideal spot for a freshly brewed cup of coffee while watching the world go by.

Fuglen: Fuglen is a must-see for a unique blend of coffee and vintage charm. It's a café as well as a gallery exhibiting mid-century

Scandinavian design. Sip your espresso while admiring the meticulously selected vintage furnishings and artwork.

Mocca Kaffebar: Mocca Kaffebar is a hidden gem in the heart of Oslo famed for its handmade coffee and scrumptious pastries. The perfume of freshly baked products fills the air, tempting you to sample the regional delicacies.

Oslo's Bars:

Himkok: Himkok, a speakeasy-style bar in Storgata, brings the handmade cocktail movement in Oslo to life. This restaurant takes pride in its innovative drinks made with locally sourced ingredients. The inviting, darkly lighted atmosphere adds to the charm.

The Thief Rooftop Bar: This rooftop bar atop The Thief Hotel is the ultimate of luxury, with panoramic views of the Oslo fjord. Sip unique cocktails and take in the gorgeous sunset while immersing yourself in the modern, art-filled environment.

Schouskjelleren Mikrobryggeri: Beer lovers will be in heaven at Schouskjelleren Mikrobryggeri. This bar, housed in a historic underground brewery, offers an outstanding assortment of craft brews. The rustic backdrop and knowledgeable employees make a welcoming environment.

Flavors from the Region:

Don't miss out on trying classic Norwegian sweets when touring Oslo's cafés and pubs. For a taste of the native food, try a slice of kringle, a sweet pastry, or some reindeer jerky. For an authentic experience, pair these treats with aquavit, a traditional Scandinavian spirit.

Chapter 4: Top 10 Outdoor Activities

As the crisp Norwegian breeze tousled my hair and the dynamic energy of Oslo surrounded me, I set out to discover the top ten outdoor activities that make this city an adventurer's delight. With a heart full of anticipation, I soon learned that Oslo offered a treasure trove of experiences for travelers seeking nature's embrace and wonderful memories.

1. Fjord Cruises: My voyage began with a fjord cruise, an awe-inspiring journey through Oslo's magnificent fjords. As I cruised along the tranquil waters, the sheer cliffs, gorgeous islands, and the magnificent Oslo Opera House came into view. The silence of the fjords, along with the gentle swaying of the boat, provided a peaceful getaway from the hectic metropolis.

2. Vigeland Park: Oslo's Vigeland Park exemplifies the city's passion for art and nature.

I went through 200 captivating Gustav Vigeland statues situated among wonderfully planted grounds. The centerpiece, the Monolith, stood towering, depicting the human journey in a complex and thought-provoking manner.

3. **Holmenkollen Ski Jump:** The thrill-seeker in me couldn't resist the Holmenkollen Ski Jump. Even in the summer, this legendary ski jump provided panoramic views of Oslo and the surrounding forests. Standing at the top, I felt a rush of excitement as I imagined the courage required to jump from that massive ramp.

4. **Hiking in Nordmarka:** A short tram trip from the city center took me to Nordmarka, a vast forested wilderness. Hiking through its well-marked pathways, I was surrounded by magnificent lakes and deep woodlands. It was a

peaceful retreat where I connected with nature and admired the simplicity of life.

5. Island Hopping: The Oslo Archipelago, with over 40,000 islands, was a wonderland waiting to be discovered. I took a ferry to the lovely islands of Hoveyda and Gressholmen. Picnicking along the beach and swimming in the crystal-clear seas made for a beautiful day in the sun.

6. riding in Oslo: Oslo is a bicycle-friendly city with several riding pathways. I rented a bike and cycled through the city's green spaces, such as Bygdy and Ekeberg Park. Cycling along the shore and through beautiful parks provided me with a fresh perspective of Oslo's splendor.

7. Kayaking in Oslofjord: For an aquatic experience, I tried kayaking in Oslofjord. Paddling beneath the blue sky, I discovered hidden coves and a different perspective on the city's shoreline. The sense of freedom and tranquility on the lake was wonderful.

8. Camping in Stmarka: I went camping in Stmarka to experience the pure essence of Norway's wilderness. I set up a tent by the tranquil Lake Yungen, cooked over an open fire, and slept beneath a star-studded sky. It was a true taste of the Norwegian outdoors.

9. Tryvann Ski Resort: During the winter months, Tryvann Ski Resort transforms into a snowy wonderland. I couldn't stop myself from strapping on some skis and floating down the slopes. The exciting rush and breathtaking vistas made this a highlight of my trip.

10. Oslo Summer Park: My adventure concluded at Oslo Summer Park, where I channeled my inner daredevil on zip lines, high ropes courses, and gigantic swings. The excitement of overcoming hurdles up in the treetops was a suitable finish to my outdoor adventures in Oslo.

Nature combines smoothly with urban life in Oslo, providing a variety of outdoor activities for tourists like me. Each experience I had was a chapter in my Norwegian trip, a tribute to the city's distinct appeal and the innumerable memories I'll remember for the rest of my life. Oslo is more than just a vacation; it's an invitation to explore, reconnect with nature, and create your own extraordinary stories amidst its stunning surroundings.

Top Attractions

Here are some must-see tourism attractions:

Vigeland Park: This world-renowned sculpture park showcases Gustav Vigeland's sculptures and is a testimony to Oslo's creative legacy.

The Viking Ship Museum: This museum, which houses superbly preserved Viking ships, provides a fascinating view into Norway's rich nautical past.

The Fram Museum: Explore the arctic exploration ship Fram and learn about Norwegian explorers like Roald Amundsen. The Munch Museum: This museum is dedicated to the works of Edvard Munch and displays some of the most recognizable pieces of Norwegian art.

Aker Brygge and Tjuvholmen: These contemporary waterfront locations are ideal for strolling, dining, and taking in the bustling environment.

The Royal Palace and Palace Park: Take a guided tour or simply observe the spectacular buildings and gardens of the Norwegian monarch's official residence.

The Nobel Peace Center: Learn about the Nobel Peace Prize and its laureates through interactive exhibitions and thought-provoking displays.

Holmenkollen Ski Museum and Tower: In addition to the famed ski jump, this complex includes a museum covering the history of skiing and winter sports.

The National Gallery: Home to a large collection of Norwegian and foreign art, including Edvard Munch's "The Scream."

Oslo Opera House: Known for its remarkable architecture, this opera house offers guided tours as well as breathtaking views of the city from its rooftop.

Safety Tips

Maintain constant awareness of your surroundings. This is especially crucial in congested locations such as tourist sites and public transportation.

- Keep your stuff near to you and be on the watch for pickpockets.

- Don't wander alone at night, especially in unknown regions. If you must walk alone, stay in well-lit places and be mindful of your surroundings.

- Avoid carrying significant sums of cash or valuables. If you must bring cash, store it in a secret pocket or a money belt.

- When you're not in your hotel room, lock the door and windows.

- When taking public transportation, keep an eye on your possessions. Do not leave your backpack alone on the floor.
- Be aware of strangers who approach you and offer you assistance or ask for money. These people could be con artists.

- If you feel unsafe, heed your instincts and leave the situation. Don't be scared to seek assistance from a police officer or security guard.

- Let someone know where you're going and when you intend to return.
- Carry a whistle or personal alarm with you.
- Dress in a way that makes you feel at ease and confident.

- Don't be afraid to decline unwelcome attention.
Remove yourself from the situation if you are uneasy.

- Keep an eye on the area near the Central Station. This is a recognized drug dealing location that can be a little sleazy.

- When taking cabs, use caution. There have been reports of taxi drivers overcharging visitors.
- If you're going trekking or camping, make sure someone knows where you're going and when you anticipate to return. Check the weather forecast and be prepared for inclement weather.

Chapter 5: Culture and History

- The Nobel Peace Center

The Nobel Peace Center, located along Oslo's scenic coastline, is a testimony to the enduring spirit of peace and human rights. This extraordinary institution is more than a museum; it is a haven of inspiration and a celebration of the hard efforts done by individuals and organizations around the world to promote peace.

The Nobel Peace Center, which was inaugurated in 2005, is a fitting monument to the Nobel Peace Prize, one of the world's most renowned honors. Since 1901, this award, founded by inventor Alfred Nobel's will, has been handed yearly in Oslo to persons who have made remarkable contributions to the cause of peace. The facility is conveniently positioned near Oslo City Hall, which hosts the Nobel

Peace Prize ceremony, making it an important component of the city's cultural environment.

Visitors are instantly struck by the spirit of reverence and hope that pervades the Nobel Peace Center. The architecture is a work of art in and of itself, with its sleek, modern style that mixes well with the historic surroundings. The exhibitions are painstakingly arranged on the inside to present a thorough picture of the laureates, their accomplishments, and the larger context of their work.

The Nobel Field, an immersive installation featuring the faces and voices of all Nobel Peace Prize laureates, is one of the most captivating parts of the institution. You'll hear their stories, see their photos, and receive insight into their incredible accomplishments as you walk through this enthralling show. It's a highly affecting experience that emphasizes the importance of their work in the pursuit of global peace.

The Nobel Peace Center also hosts temporary exhibitions that explore various aspects of peace-building, from individual laureates' tales to bigger subjects including climate change, human rights, and conflict resolution. These exhibitions demonstrate the ever-changing character of the peace movement and the numerous obstacles that people who promote it encounter.

Visitors of all ages can interact with interactive components throughout the museum. The Nobel Peace Center makes learning about peace exciting and accessible, with multimedia exhibitions that study the impact of social media on peace advocacy and interactive simulations that put you in the shoes of a peace negotiator.

The center's dedication to education extends beyond its physical boundaries. It organizes seminars, talks, and activities to encourage people to actively interact with peace concepts and values. The Nobel Peace Center has something for everyone, whether you're a student, a scholar, or just a curious traveler.

Before you leave, don't forget to stop by the Nobel Shop, which features a carefully curated assortment of books, gifts, and mementos commemorating the Nobel Peace Prize's legacy. It's the ideal spot to pick up a memorable souvenir or thoughtful gift for a loved one.

The National Gallery is a treasure trove of art and culture that I discovered as I wandered through the energetic streets of Oslo. This wonderful institution, which is tucked away in the center of the Norwegian city, is a haven for art lovers and a must-see for anyone hoping to fully appreciate the wealth of the nation's artistic legacy.

As soon as I walked into the gallery, a sense of serenity overcame me, as if I had entered a realm of timeless beauty. There was an aura of awe for the amazing collection that awaited us as the quiet whispers of other visitors filled the room. The National Gallery's stunning architecture, a fusion of classical and modern style, only to the excitement.

"The Scream," a famous picture by Edvard Munch, was prominently displayed on one wall and caught my attention right away. I was astounded by the figure's stunning hues and eerie attitude. As I stood in front of this masterwork, I couldn' help but think about how masterfully Munch had caught the depths of human feeling.

As I made my way through the gallery, I came across a wide variety of Norwegian and foreign artworks. Johan Christian Dahl's romantic landscapes, which praised Norway's natural beauty, as well as Gustav Vigeland's fascinating portraits and Harald Sohlberg's avant-garde compositions, attested to the country's rich cultural heritage.

Finding lesser-known treasures like Nikolai Astrup's stunning landscapes and Harriet Backer's ethereal interiors was one of the joys of my trip. These undiscovered gems demonstrated the range and depth of

Norwegian artistic talent. I couldn't help but feel a strong connection to Norway's past and present as I walked the hallways. The National Gallery had not only preserved art, but also the spirit of a country. A monument to the eternal power of creation, it was a trip through time and emotion.

The National Gallery in Oslo is a place where art comes to life, where history echoes in the paintbrushes, and where culture and legacy are honored in each and every artistic gesture. I wholeheartedly advise a trip to this cultural treasure to any traveler looking for a unique and enlightening experience. It is more than just a gallery; it is a journey into the very core of Norwegian creativity.

Tourists might anticipate the following when visiting The National Gallery in Oslo:

World-class Art Collection: The National Gallery is home to an outstanding collection of works by Norwegian and foreign artists. There are well-known pieces by masters like Edvard Munch, Johan Christian Dahl, and Harriet Backer that represent a wide and enthralling spectrum of aesthetic expressions.

The iconic painting "The Scream" by Edvard Munch is one of the gallery's most well-known exhibits. You can anticipate seeing this masterpiece up close and reflecting on its powerful emotional impact.

Historic and Contemporary Art: The gallery features a variety of old and new works, offering insights into Norway's artistic development throughout the centuries.

Explore a variety of art forms, including Symbolism, Expressionism, and romantic landscapes, among others. Different artistic movements and genres are represented in the gallery's collection.

Cultural Perspective: The National Gallery provides a singular look into Norwegian culture and tradition via the prism of art. You'll have a better understanding of the nation's past and current identity.

Exhibits that Teach: Many exhibits offer instructive displays and descriptions, providing both art connoisseurs and beginners with an educational experience. An atmosphere of peace and contemplation permeates the gallery, allowing visitors to take their time and enjoy the art. Reflection is encouraged by the quiet atmosphere.

Occasional Special Exhibitions: Depending on when you visit, you may have the chance to view special exhibitions or transient displays, which frequently showcase various themes and artists.

Gift store: There is frequently a gift store where you may buy artwork-related trinkets, books, and prints as a memento of your trip.

Visitor Services: The gallery typically provides visitor services including audio tours, guided tours, and educational materials to improve your knowledge of the artworks.

The National Gallery works to ensure that all visitors may use it, and it has facilities and accommodations for both families with young children and those with impairments.

Café: A few galleries feature a café where you may relax and have a drink while admiring the artwork.

Check the gallery's photography guidelines before taking pictures because some locations may only allow non-flash photography while others may not allow it at all.

Check the gallery's official website frequently for updates on its hours of operation as well as information on any upcoming events or closures.

Admission Fees: Entrance usually entails payment of a fee. Be prepared to spend, and if you want to skip the line, think about buying your tickets in advance.

The Royal Palace, located in Oslo, the charming capital of Norway, serves as a regal symbol of both the country's long history and its modern allure. Tourists are immediately enthralled by this enormous building's neoclassical magnificence as they approach it. Even for seasoned travelers, it is a sight to behold and the sense of awe is evident.

The palace, which has been keeping watch since the early 19th century, emanates a sense of nobility that instantly transports you into a fairytale. The palace is the ideal fusion of history and nature thanks to the immaculately maintained gardens that surround it, which are evidence of Norway's commitment to maintaining its natural beauty. You can't help but imagine what life would be like as royalty as you take a guided tour via its lavish rooms.

Even kings and queens can have a sense of humor, as evidenced by the yearly "Barnas Kongehus" festival where kids take over the palace for a day. Just when you start to get a little too enthralled, the guide may regale you with humorous anecdotes of odd royal traditions.

You'll experience a sense of admiration for the palace's past as well as a hint of pity for the royals who have lived there as you depart. It's a must-see for anybody experiencing Oslo, where history and humor are combined in a setting that will captivate you completely.

Considering my own experience, what can tourists expect and explore

Visitors to Oslo's Royal Palace may anticipate a compelling journey rich in tradition, culture, and scenic beauty. Expect and explore the following:

Architecturally impressive: The Royal Palace is a magnificent illustration of neoclassical design. With its columns, statues, and graceful design, the building's outer grandeur is sure to impress. Spend some time admiring the architectural features and taking pictures.

The Guard is shifted: Don't skip the daily ceremonial of the changing of the guard outside the palace. It's an interesting ritual that offers the chance to see accuracy and discipline in action.

Guided Tours: Throughout the summer, guided tours of the palace are offered. In addition to learning about the history of the palace and the Norwegian monarchy, you will also tour lavish halls and royal chambers.

Royal Park: The magnificent Slottsparken (Palace Park) surrounds the palace. This vast green area is ideal for a leisurely stroll, a picnic, or just taking in the peaceful surroundings. The park is decorated with lovely flowers in the spring.

Statues and Monuments: There are many statues and monuments in the park, notably the statue of King Karl Johan, which is a well-liked location for pictures.

Engaging History: Learn about the royal heritage of Norway, its traditions, and the monarchy's function in contemporary Norway. You'll learn about the country's past and present.

Cultural Events: Depending on when you visit, there may be cultural events or exhibitions happening within or outside the palace that give you the chance to fully experience Norwegian culture.

Panorama views of Oslo, including the city center and Oslo Fjord, may be seen from the palace's elevated position because of its scenic surroundings. It's a great location for shooting pictures and admiring the cityscape.

Relaxed Ambiance: The palace is certainly a representation of royalty, but the ambiance is warm and at the back. You'll feel a sense of kinship with the Norwegian royalty and populace.

Gift store and Café: Before or after your visit, don't forget to stop by the café for a cup of coffee or a snack and the gift store for mementos.

Visitors will gain a strong understanding for Norway's regal legacy and the magnificent surroundings after exploring Oslo's Royal Palace, which promises a blend of history, culture, and natural beauty.

With the aid of this itinerary, you can maximize your time in Oslo by taking advantage of its scenic surroundings, rich culture, and exciting attractions.

Day 1: Upon arrival, explore the city.
Early morning: Touch down at Oslo Gardermoen Airport. Check in at the accommodation of your choice.
Afternoon: To discover more about Norway's lengthy history, begin your journey by going to the Viking Ship Museum. Take a look at the Bygdoy peninsula's lovely parks.
Evening: Enjoy a seafood meal while strolling around the Aker Brygge waterfront and admiring the magnificent views of the city.

Day 2: Nordmarka hiking

Morning: Set off for a day of trekking in Oslo's enormous woodland area, Nordmarka. Depending on your degree of fitness, there are a variety of trails to select from.

Afternoon: Have a picnic in the forest or stop by a quaint cabin for some authentic Norwegian cuisine.

Evening: Go back to the city, unwind, and have dinner at a neighborhood eatery.

The Holmenkollen and Ski Museum on Day 3

Early in the day: Tour the famous Holmenkollen Ski Jump and Ski Museum. Even skiing and snowboarding are options if you go during the winter.

Explore Frognerseteren in the afternoon, a stunning location with fantastic hiking and expansive views.

In the evening, dine on Norwegian food at a mountain resort.

Oslofjord adventure on day 4

Take a boat tour of the Oslofjord in the morning. You can go fishing, sailing, or kayaking.

Afternoon: Explore the Bygdy Maritime Museum to discover Norway's maritime heritage.

In the evening, savor a seafood meal at a fjordside establishment.

Day 5: Outside Activities

Morning: Travel to Norefjell for a day of exhilarating activities like rock climbing, zip lining, and mountain biking.

Afternoon: Take a picnic lunch and explore the local natural environment.

Return to Oslo that evening, unwind, and have dinner at a quaint neighborhood restaurant.

Day 6: Cultural enquirer

Morning: Explore Edvard Munch, a well-known Norwegian artist, at the Munch Museum.

Afternoon: Explore the Oslo Opera House and go on a guided tour to discover more about its avant-garde design.

Evening: Go to the opera house to see a classical music or modern dance performance.

7th day: Island-hopping

Early in the morning, take a ferry to one of the Oslo Islands, including Hovedya, Gressholmen, or Langyene. Visit their scenic hiking trails, historic ruins, and beaches.

Afternoon: Take in a BBQ or picnic on the islands while eating seafood.

Evening: Travel back to Oslo and have a final dinner while sampling Norwegian cuisine.

The finest of Oslo's outdoor activities, cultural experiences, gastronomic delights, and scenic splendor are all included in this 7-day adventure program. It should be customized based on your preferences and the time of year you are visiting, as Oslo provides distinctive experiences all year long. In Oslo, Norway, have a memorable adventure!

The price of the top hotels in each of these locations

On the basis of my own travel experience, I can suggest some of the top hotels in Oslo, Norway, for each day of your seven-day adventure plan. Please be aware that hotel costs might fluctuate depending on the season, inventory, and room type, so it's a good idea to check current rates and availability while making travel arrangements.

Arrival and city exploration on Day

1 Recommended Hotel: The Budget Friendly
Cost: Nightly rates often begin at roughly $250.
Highlights: A luxurious waterfront hotel with breath-taking vistas and distinctive contemporary art all throughout the place.

Day 2: Walking through Nordmarka Hotel Pick: Scandic Holmenkollen Park
Cost: Nightly rates often begin at roughly $150.
Highlights: This historic hotel is close to Nordmarka and has easy access to hiking trails as well as expansive views.

Hotel Recommendation: Lysebu Hotel Day 3: Holmenkollen and Ski Museum

Price: Nightly rates begin at about $200.

Highlights: A quaint, old hotel tucked away in the woods, close to Holmenkollen and Frognerseteren.

Day 4: Oslofjord Adventure Hotel Recommendation: The Thief (again) Price Range: Nightly rates normally start at about $250.

Highlights: Return to The Thief for its beautiful riverfront location.

Day 5: Outdoor Activities Recommended Hotel: Hotel Continental Oslo Price Range: Rates start at roughly $200 per night.

Highlights: A hotel in the heart of Oslo with quick access to Norefjell for outdoor experiences.

Day 6: Cultural Exploration Hotel Suggested: Hotel Bristol Price Range: Rates start at roughly $180 per night.

Highlights: An exquisite and traditional hotel located in the center of Oslo, close to landmarks like the Munch Museum and the Opera House.

Seventh day: Island hopping hotel Hotel Radisson Blu Plaza is advised.

Cost: Nightly rates frequently begin at about $170.

Highlights: An up-to-date, cozy hotel with convenient access to the ferry ports for island hopping in the heart of the city.

These hotel suggestions span a variety of price points and aesthetics to accommodate various tastes. Remember that costs might fluctuate, and it's a good idea to reserve your lodging in advance, especially during the busiest travel seasons. Take into account any packages or special deals that hotels might be offering to make your stay better.

- Tips for Traveling in Oslo

Traveling to Oslo, Norway's capital, is an exhilarating trip filled with breathtaking natural beauty, a rich history, and a dynamic culture. Consider these thorough tips for travelers in Oslo to make the most of your visit.

1. Weather and Packing: The weather in Norway can be unpredictable. Bring layers, a waterproof jacket, and comfortable shoes even in the summer to explore the city's steep landscape.

2. Currency: The Norwegian Krone (NOK) is the local currency of Oslo. Credit cards are widely accepted, but carry some cash with you for little purchases and transportation.

3. transit: Oslo's public transit is efficient and convenient. Get an Oslo Pass for unlimited bus, tram, and ferry rides, as well as free access to several attractions.

While most Norwegians speak English effectively, learning a few simple Norwegian words can enrich your trip and demonstrate respect for the local culture.

5. Security: Oslo is regarded as one of the safest cities in the world. Nonetheless, use common judgment, especially in congested tourist locations.

6. Accommodation: There are numerous lodging alternatives in Oslo, ranging from luxury hotels to budget-friendly hostels. Book early, especially during the high summer season.

7. Attractions: Don't miss out on iconic sights like Vigeland Park, the Viking Ship Museum, and the Sydney Opera House. Consider purchasing the Oslo Pass for discounts and expedited access.

8. Museums and Galleries: Oslo is home to a plethora of world-class museums and galleries. Edvard Munch and other Norwegian painters' works can be found in the Munch Museum and the National Gallery.

9. Fjord Tours: Experience Norway's magnificent natural scenery on a fjord trip. The Oslofjord and adjacent fjords such as Naeryfjord and Geirangerfjord are popular day outings.

10. Cuisine: Sample traditional Norwegian fare such as salmon, reindeer, and brunost (brown cheese). Explore the city's broad restaurant scene for international culinary alternatives as well.

Alcohol is only sold in government-owned stores (Vinmonopolet) as well as taverns and restaurants. Because these stores have restricted hours, plan your alcohol purchases carefully.

12. Daylight: During the summer, Oslo has nearly 24 hours of daylight. To ensure a good night's sleep, use blackout curtains in your lodging.

13. Outdoor Activities: Oslo is a paradise for outdoor enthusiasts. Hiking in Nordmarka, skiing in the winter, or cycling along the city's many scenic paths are all options.

14. Sustainability: Oslo is well-known for its dedication to the environment. While exploring the city, take public transportation, recycle, and be environmentally conscious.

15. Tipping: Tipping is not required in Norway because service charges are included in the bill.

However, as a token of appreciation, it is customary to round up the amount or give a little tip.

16. Northern Lights: If you're traveling in the winter, consider heading north to enhance your chances of seeing the awe-inspiring Northern Lights.

17. Shopping: For fashion, visit Karl Johans Gate, and for local delicacies and crafts, visit Mathallen Oslo.

18. Etiquette: Learn about Norwegian customs and etiquette, such as taking off your shoes while entering a person's home and respecting personal space.

By following these suggestions, your trip to Oslo will be both memorable and enriching. Accept the city's distinct blend of modernity and natural beauty, and you'll depart with lasting memories of this enthralling Scandinavian resort.

Happy Vacation

Made in the USA
Las Vegas, NV
03 March 2024

86659135R00075